I0814449

HIDDEN HOMES OF SOUTHERN ITALY

INSPIRATIONAL HOMES UNDER THE MEDITERRANEAN SUN

MARTA GALLI

PHOTOGRAPHY BY

MIKE KARLSSON LUNDGREN

rps

RYLAND PETERS & SMALL

For David Peters

Senior designer Megan Smith
Editor Sophie Devlin
Creative director Leslie Harrington
Senior commissioning editor Annabel Morgan
Head of production Patricia Harrington

Published in 2025 by
Ryland Peters & Small
20–21 Jockey's Fields
London WC1R 4BW
and
1452 Davis Bugg Road
Warrenton, NC 27589
www.rylandpeters.com
Email: euregulations@rylandpeters.com

10 9 8 7 6 5 4 3 2 1

A CIP record for this book is available from the British Library.

US Library of Congress CIP data has been applied for.

ISBN: 978-1-78879-670-5

Printed in China

The authorised representative in the EEA is Authorised Rep Compliance Ltd., Ground Floor. 71 Lower Baggot Street, Dublin, D01 P593, Ireland
www.arccompliance.com

CONTENTS

INTRODUCTION

The southern regions of Italy, soaked in golden sunlight, have long been considered among the world's most desirable destinations. Visitors may be drawn by the mild climate, rich history and sweeping natural landscapes, but for those who decide to settle down, something more intangible comes into play. As the layered interiors featured in this book show, creating a home that feels authentic has little to do with aspirational clichés.

In one meeting, as I was trying to persuade a prospective contributor to take part in this project, he asked to see an example of the locations we were planning to include. "I like this," he said, "because it's normal."

From a publicity perspective, "normal" is far from ideal. Products must be marketed as remarkable, exclusive, aspirational. Yet I've been in hotels that were all three—and, often, I couldn't wait to leave. Of course that's a personal response. But the "normality" that photographer Mike Karlsson Lundgren and I were looking for is anything but ordinary. It's a kind of everyday that is full of grace.

In the eclectic array we've gathered—spanning a spectrum from city dwellings to rural retreats—we've stepped into homes that are sumptuous or minimalist; shaped by masculine energy or poetic softness; imbued with an atmosphere of monastic order or seductive chaos; contemplating the grand as well as the bohemian.

But no matter the style (or size), there was always some sort of intimacy; a warm and timeless quality. I guess that's the nature of a space where life finds room to unfold and leave its mark—a place that feels lived in. It would be a hazard to claim that some ways of living are more desirable than others, instead each approach offers inspiration behind closed doors.

What mattered most to us, in the making of this book and through pictures, was ensuring that every home

A cozy corner in front of the fireplace at the Puglian retreat of Ludovica Serafini and Roberto Palomba (*page 6*). Carved out of a former oil mill, the space was refurbished with respect for its historical features, such as the 17th-century vaulted ceilings, and furnished with contemporary design pieces. The refined detail of a post-war armchair reflects the understated elegance of the architecture inspired by Jean Prouvé in Federica Cimatti's holiday home, set on an agricultural plot overlooking the sea near the Vendicari nature reserve in Sicily (*page 7*). Giuseppe Amato's family home in the heart of Palermo—featuring Art Nouveau floor tiles and a mix of ancient and modernist heirlooms—is a space filled with books and memories (*below*).

conveyed a true sense of place. Many of these houses carry the imprint of their past lives—not erased, but made valuable by loving restorations. Others engage in close relationship with their surroundings, in a sort of permeability between indoors and outdoors.

The decaying grandeur of a palazzo in Naples, the farmhouse in Puglia immersed in an olive grove where inhabitants once shared space with animals, that unmistakable *Leopard* flair that could only be Sicilian—all feel like authentic experiences of the Italian south.

Some of the people featured on this journey through Puglia, Sicily and Campania were born here. They left and then returned. Others arrived with the romantic idea of starting over or establishing their own *buen retiro*. Eventually, it became increasingly central to their emotional geography.

Areas like Salento in Puglia and the Val di Noto in southeastern Sicily have in recent years become magnets for a community of expats, as they offer—in contexts framed by Baroque cities, turquoise seas, laid-back lifestyles and delicious food—either the most charming abandoned architecture or swaths of pristine land, along with the possibility of transforming these sites into dream homes, thanks to craftsmanship that continues to preserve unchanged traditions.

This book was conceived as a second chapter and a natural continuation of *Hidden Homes of Tuscany & Umbria*, in which Caroline Clifton-Mogg elegantly captured the essence of rural escapes in central Italy. The process has taken us off the beaten path, into private, often hidden realms where homes

reveal their intimate stories. As we came to understand, these stories often are woven into the collection of objects such houses cradle—for each one becomes not only a source of aesthetic pleasure but also a vessel of meaning and memories.

Add the Mediterranean setting—a cultural crossroads where traces of ancient Greek civilization mingle with Roman, Byzantine, Arab, Norman or Spanish influences. This rich layering has been absorbed into the present, and offers a wealth of possibilities for the imagination. The south can embody many things: a rural dream, a space of freedom or an escapist reverie. It is no surprise, then, that dreamers from diverse backgrounds have found here exactly what they were looking for.

The oldest part of the architecture at Palazzo Spinelli di Laurino in Naples—where Nathalie de Saint Phalle has lived since the 1990s—dates back to the 15th century (*above left*). A sculptural Dimoremilano metal seat in Luca Bombassei's *masseria* in Salento creates a bold contrast between the historical, rural setting and the contemporary furnishings with a distinctly urban flair (*above right*). A detail of the faithfully restored interiors at Villa Ruiz, just outside Noto in Sicily, and a glimpse of its striking neoclassical façade (*pages 10 and 11*).

LASTING LEGACY

Starting in the 19th century, amid political turmoil, the aristocrats and upper bourgeoisie in south-eastern Sicily built summer retreats in the rocky Iblean highlands, an area prized for its climate and game. Among them, Villa Ruiz is perhaps the most discreet, with its neoclassical façade shrouded in the vegetation of a sprawling estate.

When summer came, light clothes, furnishings and everything else needed for a seasonal sojourn were packed into heavy trunks and loaded onto carriages; cooks and servants were sent ahead. The convoy made its way uphill, cutting through the blazing landscape. But once the family reached the house, the countryside breeze would lull them into peace.

The Ruiz family acquired the estate in the 1930s. Of the eight siblings, none would end up marrying, leaving their lineage and manor without heirs. In the 1950s, one of the sisters—remembered as the most vivacious—died suddenly of an illness, and the fine summer days were soon over. They never returned to the house, which settled into a life of seclusion.

Fifty years on, Corrado Papa, an architect from Noto, visited the house. Everything was just as the last occupants had left it: silver flatware in the drawers, the gramophone still working. The property had become a target for real-estate speculation, but Corrado, who was very close to the last surviving members of the family, was determined to save it. He thought of Jean-Louis Remilleux, with whom he was then working on the monumental restoration of Palazzo Castelluccio in the heart of Noto. Perhaps the French television producer didn't need another house, but he had the right sensibility.

"I fell in love with this part of Sicily, and I wanted to live here," Jean-Louis recounts. "When the architect came to me, I agreed—it was a good idea to have a retreat in the hills, where the summers are more tolerable." Corrado introduced him to the family's last descendant: "An old Sicilian woman, dressed in black. She was looking for someone who would respect the history of this place. I promised her the name would remain unchanged."

"The restoration at Villa Ruiz was carried out with the intent to preserve its *Leopard*-esque flair," says Corrado,

referring to the famous novel by Giuseppe Tomasi di Lampedusa. "We were careful not to erase the signs of time or give the façade a Botox job. We stripped the interiors of 20th-century additions and added only the essential utility systems, all discreetly concealed."

On the ground floor, a room that had been sacrificed to create a garage was reintegrated into the original plan and embellished with a trompe l'œil depicting a winter garden. This allowed for the recovery of the building's Palladian symmetry, with four rooms on the ground level and four above, all opening onto the central hall.

In a meticulous restoration, Corrado reinstated the original *pietra pece* floors—a dark, bitumen-laced limestone—replacing the speckled marble tiles laid during the 1950s. Elsewhere, period cementine and glazed ceramic tiles from Caltagirone and Santo Stefano di Camastra were either preserved or carefully reintroduced. The double staircase, once simplified, was rebuilt in accordance with the original design. Corrado made full use of local craftsmen's skills—people who still know how to work in the old-fashioned way. Upstairs, the old kitchen—with its cistern and hearths once used to heat water—has been repurposed as a bathroom.

"Villa Ruiz had a lot of charm—even when it was completely empty. Everything felt authentic. I didn't want to overdo it, as some *décorateurs* sometimes do. Everything we brought into the house could have been born here," continues Jean-Louis. "I like traveling to Sicily by car. I drive down from the south of France—first Genoa, then Florence, Rome, Naples. Then we put the car on the boat and arrive in Palermo. I stop at all the antiques dealers along the way. And if I find anything typical of the South, especially Sicilian, I buy it."

Jean-Louis has furnished the rooms with an eclectic mix of 19th-century furniture, *wunderkammer* curiosities and paintings reminiscent of the Grand Tour era. He says he's become a sort of guide to the area when friends visit, although they're all perfectly happy to stay at home. "We hang around the pool, we read under the Australian banyan trees, or—if the weather isn't good—we stay in the cinema room and watch old movies," he says.

In the garden, jasmine, cacti and other exotic species are grown near the house, while olive and almond trees stretch across the rolling hills, blending into the landscape. On one of the terraces, the dark waters of the pool reflect the sky and the tall palm trees.

Today, moving through this space feels like a time-warp safari—and you can imagine its owner enjoying a 19th-century lifestyle. "Sometimes I really need to escape the present, which I think has somehow lost its sense of beauty. This is my parenthesis in the past. *Mon refuge*," says Jean-Louis.

"Here I've tried to recreate the atmosphere of a Sicilian house as if this were the house of my Sicilian grandmother—but of course, it's just a fantasy."

Set on the Iblean plateau in the Contrada of San Corrado di Fuori, Villa Ruiz has the austere presence of a fortress. The foyer features a load-bearing barrel vault constructed with rubble stone and plaster over formwork (*page 12*). In the salon, a trompe l'œil by Alexandrine Stordeur depicts the island's lush flora—banana trees, agaves, araucarias and palms—nodding to the 19th-century fashion for the exotic in garden design (*pages 13 and 14)*. A rare example of neoclassical architecture in the area, the building is marked by a recessed upper-floor loggia and framed by two monumental *Ficus macrophylla* trees (*page 15*). The furnishings in the salon reflect a layered 19th-century taste for eclecticism, with inlaid Sicilian pieces that would be perfectly at home in Giuseppe Tomasi di Lampedusa's *The Leopard*, and the lighter touch of a polychrome glazed jardinière (*right*).

In the foreground, a hand-embroidered cloth covers the dining table, supporting a blown-glass decanter in early 20th-century Italian Liberty style (*above*). A view of the dining room, where the vaulted ceiling has been painted with trompe-l'œil coffered panels by Alexandrine Stordeur (*opposite*). The neoclassical-style armchairs are Italian. Laid during the most recent restoration, the floor is made of late 18th-century Sicilian tiles sourced from an antiques dealer in Palermo.

le Parrain
Albert S Ruddy
Titanus
IL GATTOPARDO

The only room that reveals we are not, in fact, still in the 19th century, is the TV lounge, which is hung with framed movie posters in a nod to the homeowner's passion for classic cinema (*opposite*). A series of volcanic paintings—Vesuvius above all—reflects a recurring theme in travel art during the Grand Tour era (*above*). These works are part of a larger collection dedicated to the genre. The stools are upholstered in a modern fabric reinterpreting chinoiserie motifs (*right*). One of four bedrooms, all opening onto the first-floor central salon, is furnished with a pair of mahogany four-posters bought in Turin (*pages 22 and 23*). The floral cementine tiles are original, while the neoclassical wallpaper is by Atelier d'Offard, specialists in historical re-editions. Portuguese wooden chairs complete the room.

SAGO

Located above the kitchen, this upstairs room still preserves the original water inlet connected to the underground cistern, along with the hearths once used to heat it—complete with typical lidded copper containers (*opposite and this page*). Today, the space has been transformed into a bathroom with a copper tub. When the house was purchased, there was no electricity; the renovation by architect Corrado Papa made it possible to install the necessary modern systems while keeping them discreetly hidden.

What is presumed to have been the original master bedroom, complete with an alcove and separate service room access—one for her, one for him (*above left, above and left*). One of the villa's most theatrical bedrooms, marked by a distinct Empire style (*opposite*). The space is furnished with a gilded wooden bed topped by an elaborate carved mirror, both dating to the late 18th century. The wallpaper echoes the decorative motif of the bed's columned headboard and the floor tiles are early 19th-century. The room is dedicated to French general Joachim Murat, Napoleon's right-hand man and husband of Caroline Bonaparte, who became King of Naples.

In the first-floor salon, the golden goffré wallpaper by Atelier d'Offard glows, contrasting with the inky *pietra pece* floor to sumptuous effect (*opposite and above*). A 19th-century Sicilian sofa and decorative objects add flavor to the space. Glimpses of the first-floor loggia, an extension of the salon, offering views toward the sea (*pages 30 and 31*). During World War II, Villa Ruiz was requisitioned by the German command due to its strategic position.

WILD RETREAT

From the hill you look down over the Sicilian countryside stretching to the coastal reserve of Vendicari—a lush green valley in winter, golden and dotted with Mediterranean maquis in summer. The landscape is wild in appearance, yet has been shaped by human activity since ancient times. There a modern structure stands alone, rising from the soil.

Years ago, Federica Cimatti, an art and architecture editor living in Milan, set out to buy a piece of land and build her dream house in Sicily. She had spent many summers in this area; for a time she even lived in a small cottage inside the nature reserve—without electricity, which is restricted in the protected *Oasi Faunistica* (wildlife oasis).

Before finding this spot on the rural outskirts of Noto, she had been hunting intensely for the right plot to settle on—but nothing ever felt quite right. "I was shown all sorts of ruins and parcels of land, but there was always something off. I'd spot a construction or something disruptive getting in the way." She was about to give up when the real estate agent called again. "There's actually one more," he said, "although there's a high chance it won't work—you know, it's complicated."

What was complicated, it turned out, was the location. It was by no means easy to reach: a narrow, exceptionally bumpy lane wound through farmers' fields, crossed a small stream and led to a remote, terraced clearing. There was nothing there but an old *aia*—a flat, circular surface typically found near a rural dwelling, once used for threshing grain. Federica concluded her house should be on the same level as the *aia*, which would later become her outdoor space: part dining area, part solarium. And that was it.

She had already admired the work of Sicilian architect Maria Giuseppina Grasso Cannizzo in *Casabella* magazine, and they had quite a few friends in common. The pair met at Maria Giuseppina's seaside retreat. "I felt like I was the one who had to pass the test," Federica recalls. After that meeting, they visited the site together. "She was struck by the beauty of

The modernist structure is an international RIBA award-winning project by Maria Giuseppina Grasso Cannizzo, known as FCN 2009 (*pages 32 and 33*). It stands on a slope, surrounded by carob, olive, almond and mastic trees—species typical of the Mediterranean maquis. Inside, antique hand-painted Sicilian ceramics are lined up on a mid-century String wall unit in teak (*above*). Around the custom-designed dining table, the distinctive silhouette of Arne Jacobsen's Series 7 chair for Vitra stands out alongside the austere rigor of Egon Eiermann's SE 68 for Wilde + Spieth—a classic of functional design (*opposite*).

the place." Standing there, facing the azure line of sea on the horizon, Federica explained: "I only have two requirements. That it be built right here"—she said, opening her arms to form a cross—"and that it is clad in wood."

A few months later, she drove to Maria Giuseppina's office in Vittoria, where a 1:20 scale model of the project awaited her. It's safe to say Federica had no faint idea of what to expect, but she was thrilled by what she saw. Amid a sea of papers sat a toy-like structure—a cross between an American mobile home and the "demountable" houses of the rationalist tradition, in the spirit of Jean Prouvé. It had a compact volume, with a movable section that slid along two tracks to reveal a wide veranda. The project would later go on to receive a RIBA Award for Architectural Excellence in 2012.

When the construction began, prefabricated pieces were used to overcome the difficulties of the site, but the road still had to be enlarged. Today, the architecture peeks out unexpectedly from behind the olive and carob trees of this pastoral setting, resting on large concrete trestles designed to negotiate the site's steep slope and allow runoff water to flow beneath the house. On the day of our visit, after heavy spring rains, the gorse bushes were in bloom, as was the tall white asphodel. A carpet of *Sulla glomerata* covered the usually bare terrain leading to the pool on the terrace above.

The structure is oriented toward the sea, with a glass wall that gives the impression not just of looking at the landscape, but of belonging to it—all while remaining inside. The living room, kitchen and bedroom are in the main block, while two guest rooms sit in the movable section. The interior is a calm, functional space punctuated by a pared-back, carefully curated selection of modernist and postwar pieces. There's nothing superfluous or overly ornate, yet Federica has a fondness for collecting ceramic and metal boxes from the Bauhaus era. "This was a pastry tin, and that one was used to store bread."

Not far from the house lives a farmer, who planted a special kind of tomato just for her and looks after the three cats she adopted whenever she's away. When it's time to leave, the house shuts down: the pivoting panels come together, and the guest-room box slides along tracks on the terrace. "Thankfully, Maria Giuseppina doesn't like complicated technology—opening and closing are simple gestures. It's a matter of mechanics." That's when the "magic box" becomes an unassailable fortress, waiting for its owner to return.

A view of the minimalist kitchen island, made of Corian with an antique Sicilian bowl for contrast (*opposite*). Suspended above it is a sculptural STR02 lamp by Maurizio Navone for RESTART/MILANO. The pantry is cleverly concealed behind the wall. Purposefully raised off the ground on concrete trestles, the house offers a spectacular view across the Vendicari Nature Reserve to the coastline beyond—one of Federica's main requests was to be able to see the sea (*above*).

Federica furnished the interiors with a symphony of understated pieces, mostly from the postwar period, such as the 1970s vintage sofa, Tolomeo floor lamp by Artemide and 1950s armchairs by Antonio Gorgone (*pages 38–39 and opposite*). From the front door, there's a glimpse of the old threshing floor, which is now an outdoor living room. Carefully selected items include a 1960s Swedish trolley, a vintage glass fruit bowl and a side table by Ignazio Gardella (*above, above right and right*).

The main bedroom has a pared-back layout, but the view opening out onto the endless countryside creates a sumptuous effect (*above*). The many large windows not only blur the boundary between indoors and out but also allow for excellent air circulation. The BRS03 lamp beside the bed is by Maurizio Navone for RESTART/MILANO (*right*). Federica bought the large mid-century armoire on eBay before the house was even designed, so the architect decided to plan the room around it (*opposite*).

Outside, an industrial Orsogril steel structure creates a terrace that reveals the ground below (*opposite*). A Marni lounge chair—handmade in Colombia—sits in front of the movable section of the house that houses the guest bedrooms. The bathroom features a steel shower tray that opens to the outside and also serves as a transitional space (*above*).

The house is clad in marine-grade okoume plywood panels (*this page*). Known for its resistance to moisture and weather, this material evokes the world of nautical construction and reinforces the building's connection to its natural surroundings. A key design element visible here is the distinctive slope of the roof, which opens like a telescope toward the horizon to amplify the view of the landscape. The system of folding panels, along with the movable section on tracks that houses the two guest bedrooms, allows the house to be fully sealed when unoccupied.

TREASURE TROVE

The American art historian and curator Peter Benson Miller is an old-world aesthete with unusually eclectic tastes. He arrived in the Salento region of Puglia from Rome, where he and his Italian partner Giovanni Panebianco had been living in an apartment crammed with his motley collection, and was looking for a place to call home.

Peter has always been inclined to surround himself with beautiful things, ever since his teens when he and his parents would rummage in antiques fairs and country-estate auctions. During a house-hunting tour, he and Giovanni (a civil servant and president of the Premio Paganini violin competition) stopped in the small town of Giuggianello. At the threshold of a stone townhouse, they couldn't have guessed that it would open into a hidden garden, just big enough to conjure a diminutive Eden.

The dust-laden interiors looked forlorn, but in some rooms, colorful 19th-century tiles—laid in a carpet-style design with floral and geometric patterns—had survived intact. That settled it. Soon they came to realize, however, that to complete or redo other, less well-preserved floors would be daunting. It was later, on a trip to Lebanon, that they stumbled upon what they needed—a reclamation yard overflowing with similar tiles and slabs of Carrara marble, shipped from Italy a century earlier.

Back in Puglia, they bought a smaller adjacent property and began the work of restoration by enlarging a courtyard between the two houses. This would make a more airy, harmonious space and link the labyrinthine array of buildings. During the process, an elaborate arch—recalling Venetian façades—emerged from a wall that divides what is now the kitchen from the dining room. "It may date to the 18th century, as the quarry that produced this *pietra leccese* [the local limestone] was closed in 1733," says Peter, explaining that it stands as proof that this area, once known as Terra d'Otranto—its stones still bearing the imprint of the Turkish conquest in 1480—was a crossroads of cultures. "The startling blend of Byzantine forms, Latin rite

churches and neo-Moorish, whimsical architecture brought me here, to the easternmost spot I could find on the Italian peninsula."

Peter's interest in the East traces back to his studies in Orientalist painting between the US and Paris, and even further to his childhood travels to Turkey, where he continued to go after earning his doctorate. Thus influenced, he and Giovanni have installed a swimming pool inspired by those found in Islamic gardens, a Moroccan-tiled fountain in the courtyard and reclaimed faucets/taps and basins from hammams in Istanbul. The ultimate decision was to name the house Beylik—a nod to the territories governed by a Bey (chieftain) during the Ottoman Empire, but not without humor.

One can read the house's name in tiny letters at the entrance, beside the door fitted with a hand-shaped knocker that was sourced during a vacation in Greece. Hundreds of pieces the couple brought back from travels, received as gifts or inherited have found their way into this house. "Probably everything else will arrive too, sooner or later," Peter says, referring to what remains in Rome.

He has put together a somehow dandified interior and spread his collection throughout the rooms. There are hand-painted ceramics from Vietri, mantel vases in the style of Constance Spry and paintings with an Orientalist flair. One—painted by the director of the Academy of Fine Arts in Hama and depicting the Syrian city before it was destroyed in 1982—is among his most treasured. "I get enamored with the story of objects," Peter muses.

There are also some eccentric series: artists' palettes hanging in the sitting room, an array of religious pictures in a guest room and prints of Mary, Queen of Scots on the walls of a tiny WC. And then there is contemporary art—by Tristano di Robilant, Tomaso De Luca, F. Taylor Colantonio, Namsal Siedlecki and other friends who might come to visit. "I like to keep it in the tradition of country houses with people coming and going."

With the same collector's instinct, Peter has filled the garden with phormium, Mediterranean spurge, lavender-cotton, roses and box balls grown from tiny sprigs taken from his mother's garden. He has recovered not only an exquisite—at times exotic—dream but perhaps the lost garden of his boyhood.

In the dining room, with its original floor and custom star-vaulted ceiling, the Pantheon table by Mario Bellini for Cassina is teamed with Basket chairs by Gian Franco Legler (*page 48*). A Gothic arch adorned with *Wisteria sinensis* frames the entrance to the back garden (*page 49*). Diverse artworks cluster around an early 20th-century sofa in the sitting room (*opposite*). These include a Peruvian Madonna brought back by Peter's great-great-uncle, an Orientalist portrait and a landscape depicting old Hama in Syria. Outside, a raised pool reflects the sculpture *Savant* by Leonid Lerman surrounded by *Rosa* x *odorata* 'Mutabilis', *Euphorbia characias* and *Helleborus argutifolius* (*above*).

The ceramics laid out in the kitchen include a 1930s Vietri sul Mare plate, a light blue bowl from a bazaar in Muscat and a blue-and-white Robert Picault piece from the 1950s (*this page*). An ancient arch, once hidden inside a wall, now frames the entrance to this room where a series of Moroccan bowls is displayed on a shelf (*opposite*). The hanging lamp was designed by Michele De Lucchi for Produzione Privata.

The library has an extendable table with a Sputnik-style pendant overhead (*this page*). On the wall, a portrait of Peter's grandmother by her aunt Anna Ingersoll is surrounded by Italian ceramics (*opposite*). The large textile vase sculpture by F. Taylor Colantonio draws inspiration from Chinese porcelain seen in a John Singer Sargent painting.

SALENTO MODERNO
IRAN

The house is full of treasures, including a sculpture by Tommaso De Luca and a canvas by Viola Yesiltac (*opposite above left*), Vietri sul Mare ceramics (*above right*) and a Tulu rug from Anatolia (*below left*). One corner has a plaster foot model and Carin Goldberg's embroidered fabric balls with motifs from Giorgio Morandi and Philip Guston (*below right*). In the sitting room, 19th-century tiles contrast with Marcel Breuer's modernist Wassily chairs (*this page*). A Fratino desk, once belonging to Giovanni's mentor, now displays an architectural model and lamps repurposed from church candelabra.

YES
WE
CAN

The enfilade that begins with the sitting room ends with two guest bedrooms that face the garden. In the first of these, a fluffy Anatolian Tulu rug lies at the foot of the Suzani-covered bed (*opposite*). Hanging on the wall is a triptych by Giuseppe Stampone, a former fellow at the American Academy in Rome during Peter's tenure as arts director. Made with a BIC pen, it depicts Barack Obama and Martin Luther King Jr. The velvet bergère is a family piece (*this page*).

The master bedroom has a Federal-style early 19th-century bed from Peter's parents' country house (*opposite*). His portrait by Illia Barger, in a style reminiscent of the Bloomsbury Group, hangs on the wall. In the second guest room of the enfilade, the pillow on the bed is made of fabric from Uzbekistan (*left*). The Qajar-style painting was found at a shop in Rome. On the secretaire sits a 1950s Murano glass aquarium by Alfredo Barbini. Another bedroom features blue stencil faux boiserie by F. Taylor Colantonio and a portrait of Francesco Clemente by Giuseppe Stampone (*below left*). Back in the master bedroom, a silverpoint portrait of Giovanni by Victor Koulbak hangs on the wall by a French wicker armchair (*below*).

This bedroom, in the oldest part of the house, has remained almost untouched, including the colorful floor tiles (*above*). Around the headboard is a collection of religious portraits, a staple of Italian folklore. The bedspread is from Fabindia. The bathroom is clad in reclaimed Carrara marble, each slab bearing on its reverse the name of the quarry and the address of its original owner in Lebanon (*right and opposite*). The faucets/taps and carved basin were sourced from a hammam, while the cast-iron tub was found on the streets of Rome.

INNER BEAUTY

At first, it didn't seem a welcoming place. The old mill, which once produced oil for lamps, was a fire-blackened fortress shrouded in darkness. But the architect's eye can picture magic where others cannot. Ludovica Serafini and Roberto Palomba have made this once-monolithic space a play of volumes and voids, concealed by an unassuming door.

The entrance could easily be missed in the labyrinth of alleys in the small town of Sogliano Cavour, in the southern reaches of Puglia known as Salento, where winding streets open unexpectedly into small squares. One step brings you inside.

The abode unfolds around a courtyard like a tiny village encircling its *piazza*. It serves both as passageway and an open-air living room that brings the light in and glows as evening falls. A few steps down, the interiors soar with the solemnity of a cathedral, showing vaulted ceilings and portions of exposed walls in creamy *pietra leccese*. Atop the structure, a rooftop annexe for guests and a series of terraces at varying levels extend across the building. Tucked away just outside the historic walled boundaries of Sogliano Cavour, from here you can look out over the old town. "The house faces inward," says Ludovica. "For the view, you must climb up to the terraces. This makes it an incredibly intimate place."

This is what the couple calls their *buen retiro*. It provides a retreat from the hectic pace of Milan, where they run their firm Palomba Serafini. Ludovica and Roberto met at a ball when they were students, they fell for each other—though it took her eight months to realize he was the only one she could marry—and eventually left Rome for Northern Italy. Some dozen years ago, while searching for a fixed holiday destination, they followed a close acquaintance who believed the old mill was something they had to see. After five intense months of renovation, they could finally start to treat Puglia as their backyard. Now they can simply board a plane whenever they feel the need to unplug.

"Converting a utilitarian structure into a home has been a fascinating and mysterious journey," Ludovica says. The larger area became the living room—an airy, open space suffused with light descending from skylights and

William Kentridge
William Kentridge
ADI
12 · RESTAURI

clerestory windows—while the sleeping quarters were carved into almost monastic alcoves for their daughter and numerous guests. "We are never alone here; the house is always full of friends. Each one finds their spot as if guided by unseen forces and sticks to it. But when someone enters the kitchen, well, it becomes a real magnet—one never gets to finish preparing a meal alone."

Taking advantage of the original flooring with its varying levels, the architects designed a separate elevated kitchen under a barrel vault. Across the living area is the master bedroom, with a mirrored armoire/wardrobe that conceals the bathroom behind it. A stone bathtub has been installed where the manger for the mill's donkeys once stood. No door was needed, but the omission caused an uproar when the builders realized it was deliberately left out. "Word spread, and soon the entire village came to see."

The whole space is furnished with understatement, blending simple, disciplined and minimal pieces of their own design with a few objects that belonged to their families, such as a collection of ceramics made by Roberto's Sardinian aunt, Emilia Palomba. The cheerful restraint of the decor leaves enough space for life to unfold naturally. As Roberto explains: "We didn't want to impose any aesthetic ideology; the site fell into place almost by necessity, designed around the people who inhabit it."

All the building asked for was its beauty to be unearthed. "When we arrived, it bore the weight of an age of pain and suffering," he recalls. "Mills like this were completely sealed structures. Those condemned to work here were like prisoners, deprived of sunlight for months." Yet the pair was not deterred, immediately recognizing the charm of the *genius loci* in this region, a vestige of ancient times when it was under Greek influence. The wine is excellent, the local music enthralling and the boys and girls could almost have been sculpted in bronze. Architecture followed suit. "This place was crying out for redemption and longing for joy. We allowed light in, we brought friendship and we have filled it with laughter."

The spacious living room has vaulted ceilings and whitewashed walls with exposed areas of honey-hued *pietra leccese* stone (*pages 64 and 65*). A mirrored door from the bedroom reflects a Lama armchair, customized in straw as a birthday gift for Roberto, and a Zen side table. Palomba Serafini's mahogany Zen screen for Exteta alongside their sofas and coffee tables for Zanotta create an understated ensemble. Their minimal Loto and Ninfea tables for Zanotta and Hiray chair for Kartell complete the setting (*opposite*). The daybed is a favorite spot for guests (*above*).

The architects designed a stripped-down chimney: its hood disappears into the wall, while the flame at floor level "evokes the primal intimacy of ancient hearths" (*this page*). Balancing nonchalance and rigor, the Paraggi sun loungers in front of it were designed for Exteta and crafted in mahogany with dove-gray fabric. The rug, also designed by the couple, was made to measure by Karpeta (*opposite*).

A short flight of steps connects the large indoor living space to the outdoors (*opposite*). The windows were crafted by local blacksmiths. The patio, reminiscent of a Moroccan riad, is furnished with selected pieces: a Piaffe bench and coffee table for Driade with a few succulents in terracotta vases (*this page*). A natural gathering spot, this open-air room features a lighting system that makes it glow at night.

In the main bedroom, Tessitura Calabrese covers add to the monastic charm (*this page*). The flooring, made of local *chianca* stone, was salvaged from the oil mill. A bathtub in the same stone, created in collaboration with Pimar, has been installed where a manger once stood (*opposite*).

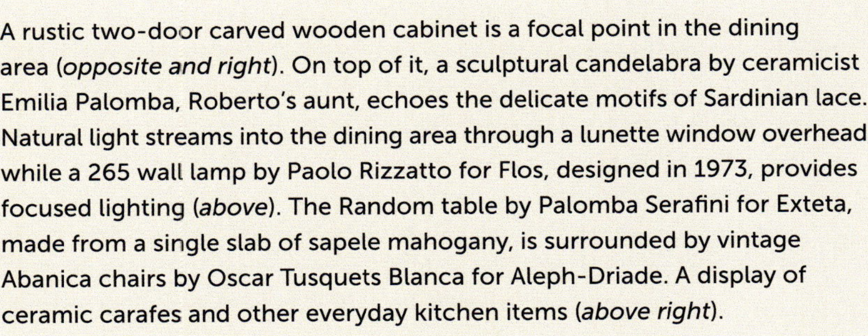

A rustic two-door carved wooden cabinet is a focal point in the dining area (*opposite and right*). On top of it, a sculptural candelabra by ceramicist Emilia Palomba, Roberto's aunt, echoes the delicate motifs of Sardinian lace. Natural light streams into the dining area through a lunette window overhead, while a 265 wall lamp by Paolo Rizzatto for Flos, designed in 1973, provides focused lighting (*above*). The Random table by Palomba Serafini for Exteta, made from a single slab of sapele mahogany, is surrounded by vintage Abanica chairs by Oscar Tusquets Blanca for Aleph-Driade. A display of ceramic carafes and other everyday kitchen items (*above right*).

On the rooftop, the guest annexe opens onto panoramic terraces accessible via an external staircase. Here, a compact kitchen features burners integrated into the countertop, while the wall showcases a fish-shaped motif from the My Décor collection, designed by the architects for Ceramica Sant'Agostino (*above left*). A Canadian red cedar bench from the Zen line for Exteta adds warmth. The Diabolo pendant was designed by Achille Castiglioni for Flos. A vibrant mix of colorful Individual Mini Round stools, from another collection designed for Exteta, pairs with the foldable Paraggi loungers (*above right*). A repurposed fishing net, used as a canopy, casts delicate shadows over the terrace, creating the perfect setting for an *aperitivo* (*opposite*).

The highest terrace is used for yoga and Pilates (*this page*). It overlooks both the historic heart of Sogliano Cavour and the patio below, where a striking *Euphorbia canariensis* stretches up to the rooftop. Salvaged from a local garden, the plant had to be lowered into the property by crane. The Indian fig cactus is similarly well adapted to the arid climate.

CHANGE OF PLAN

The Sicilian town of Modica is famous for its chocolate as well as for its countless Baroque churches that cling to the hillside, seeming to defy gravity. In the upper part of this settlement, where the built environment gives way to the countryside, lies the home of Antonino Nicastro. Once a summer refuge for his family, it is now home to him and his partner Lella Bucello.

The property originally consisted of two parts: one a limestone house, the other a tuff shed. In 2018, Antonino and Lella—both Sicilian by birth, though living in Milan at the time—decided to restore the property for their retirement years. But first the sale of Antonino's company, then the arrival of the pandemic shifted the course of their plans. Today, while Lella continues teaching and Antonino has resumed his profession, now based in Sicily, they have embraced the island's slower pace of life.

When it came time to craft a rescue plan for the house and the shed that was once used for livestock, they turned to Sicilian architect Maria Giuseppina Grasso Cannizzo. The couple felt drawn to her work, and Antonino shares her passion for collecting contemporary art.

Restoration can often present a conundrum between what to preserve and what to alter. "Maria Giuseppina would have preferred to save the old barn," Antonino says, "but since it lacked a foundation, she decided to construct a new wing that echoed its form and color using concrete, so as not to erase the memory of the place." Antonino remembers how his father, who ran a restaurant in Modica with his mother, used to come up here

Where the animal shed once stood, a newly built concrete structure echoes the shape and color of the original tuff construction (*pages 80–81*). This forms the heart of the new house: a spacious, open-plan area interrupted by two additional concrete volumes housing the bedroom, bathroom and utility spaces. The overall layout includes both covered and open-air areas. An artwork by Rossana Taormina stands on the desk (*below*). Another corner of the living area with a 1970s DS-31 leather sofa by De Sede and a throw by Society (*opposite*). The kilim rug is a Cirpi from Kurdistan, bought at Altai Gallery in Milan, while the floor lamp is the Mantis BS1 by Bernard Schottlander.

whenever he could. On holidays, the family gathered at the house and set long tables starting at 11am for lunches that stretched well into the afternoon.

The house where Antonino and Lella live today could perhaps be described as a brutalist structure grafted onto a rural dwelling to make a surprisingly harmonious whole. Surrounded by a gravel garden of olive and citrus trees, and pillows of drought-tolerant species such as *Phlomis*, *Artemisia*, *Cistus* and *Helichrysum*, it opens to the landscape through wide panes of glass.

The heart of the home is in the new structure: an open space for the living room and kitchen, with the main bedroom and utilities remaining hidden. As for the limestone house, it underwent a conservative restoration to accommodate the study and guest room. The roof was rebuilt using a traditional *incannucciato* (wattle-and-daub) technique and the floor paved with black Sicilian tiles, maintaining a clear distinction between the two wings. The owners finished the interiors with sparse yet carefully considered furniture chosen primarily for its functionality, including vintage pieces and rustic farmhouse tables that have always been there.

Antonino chose to leave the concrete walls bare, gathering his collection of paintings and photographs in the old house. "I consider the architecture a work of art in itself," he says. "This way, I can better appreciate the texture left by the reclaimed lumber."

In her design, Maria Giuseppina took into account not only Antonino and Lella's wishes, but also kept their beagle Romeo in mind. She traced a network of paths around the house and its courtyards, so he could patrol the perimeter without losing sight of his owners through the large windows. "Romeo is no longer with us, but he's buried on the slope just above the house," says Lella. "And even from there, he still keeps an eye on us."

The kitchen strikes a quietly modern note within the open-plan living space—conceived to mirror the sociable rhythm of Antonino and Lella, who love guests to gather round as they cook (*right*). The layout flows seamlessly from kitchen to dining to living area, encouraging easy conversation and conviviality. Overhead, a pair of 1920s iron pendant lamps, salvaged from an American laundry, was found at an antiques dealer. To the right stands a row of original DSC 106 desk chairs, designed in the 1960s by Giancarlo Piretti for Castelli (later Anonima Castelli).

Another view of the living room and its views over the landscape (*above*). In the foreground, the dining area features mid-century Basket chairs by Gian Franco Legler for Bonacina and a Toio floor lamp by Achille and Pier Giacomo Castiglioni for Flos. The seating includes DSC 106 chairs by Giancarlo Piretti for Castelli and a handcrafted wooden bench (*left and opposite*). The textured concrete walls of the extension retain the imprint of the reclaimed boards used during casting. Beyond the structural join connecting the new building to the old stone house is Antonino's studio, furnished with a 1940s desk he has carried with him from house to house and a desk chair by Charles and Ray Eames (*page 88*). Sicilian ceramic floor tiles demarcate the old house and the wooden doors are original (*page 89*). The armchair is the Minuetto by Plinio il Giovane.

WA
IS
OV
IF YOU WA
Love and Peace from

BACON
HOPPER
KILIM
Giappone
WORLD PRESS PHOTO

The guest room, also used as a studio by Lella, features a headboard made from a bent iron railing salvaged from the old stable (*opposite*). The artworks on the wall are by Adelita Husni-Bey, Moira Ricci, Eva Koťátková, Petrit Halilaj, Giovanni De Lazzari, Marianna Christofides, Amir Yatziv and Daniela Ortiz. The lamp beside the bed is the Tolomeo by Artemide. The antique ceramic water pitchers (*quartara*) are from Caltagirone (*above*).

BOTANICA URBANA

The house is composed of enclosed volumes, courtyards and roofless walkways that frame the interior space. The main bedroom is just large enough for the essentials and sits in a cube enclosed by a curtain made from rustic linen grain sacks (*opposite*). The black-and-white photograph by the bed shows the homeowner, captured by Carlo Ottaviano Casana. One of the open areas features a low sink and the same concrete flooring used indoors (*this page*).

This courtyard, visible from the living room, was once used for livestock and enclosed by a low wall. The olive tree, which was there when Antonino was a child, has been preserved (*above*). This is one of two courtyards in the new building, which was conceived as a structure of solids and voids. Typically Sicilian ceramic and olive-wood bowls (*right*). A view of the garden, a project by garden designer Federica Raggio; in the foreground is a lemon tree, rock roses and irises (*opposite*). Looking back at the house from the garden (*pages 96–97*).

MODERN HISTORY

It was a clear day in autumn when Paola Moscardino and Nino Filotico first laid eyes on a perfectly proportioned apartment in the heart of Lecce—Salento's Baroque city, where grand architecture meets provincial allure. Though housed in a traditional *palazzo*, it has an unpolished, authentic charm that appealed to them immediately.

The building, constructed between the 16th and 19th centuries, is set just behind the triumphal arch that once welcomed travelers from Naples. "This is a historic dwelling with its ups and downs," says Paola. "But that day, when we stepped into a lofty sitting room flooded with sunlight, we just knew."

Paola, a journalist, and Nino, founder of Filotico and Partners architects, have been living here for about 15 years with their two sons, Gabriele and Giovanni. They divide their time between this apartment and "the other house"—a grand *palazzo* in the region that has been in Nino's paternal family for generations, where they spend summers and other holidays. While they inhabit the latter with the feeling of being custodians of its legacy, this apartment seems to have been built for them. "This is an intimate home," Nino says. "Indeed, it was never meant to be formal." Although one might assume that he, as an architect, has left his mark on it, he shies away from the idea. Instead, he describes it as "a mix of things that have come together, each carrying meaning for us."

The classic enfilade—a double row of spaces anchored by the sitting room—keeps bedrooms, the kitchen and service areas discreetly tucked away. "You enter on one side, take a long circular walk and return to where you started," Paola explains. "All the little doors and hidden rooms along the way can be disorienting for visitors, which is rather amusing."

They changed little upon arrival—reopening or closing doors, glazing the floor with resin where the terrazzo had worn away, deepening the walls with muted colors and composing the interiors from the ground up. "This is not a home that has always been here, yet it wasn't exactly

In Nino's studio, an Art Deco-style loveseat stands beneath a wooden panel that has developed unique golden hues—now displayed as a painting (*page 98 below*). A red lacquered Spanish Sant'Anna chair from the 18th century, with silver carvings and a Vienna straw seat, stands in the vestibule (*page 98 above*). The entrance to the apartment (*page 99*). In the sitting room, a Raffles sofa by Vico Magistretti for De Padova brings vibrant color (*opposite*). A classic of 1960s Italian design, the Nesso lamp by Giancarlo Mattioli for Artemide stands next to a minimalist artwork made by Nino using plaster and chisel (*below right*).

designed either," Nino reflects. Family heirlooms have found their place alongside old furniture recently collected—he is a habitué of antiques markets. The dining table, a massive, austere early 19th-century piece, was found at a church rummage sale and simply rewaxed. "I would never erase the signs of age—who knows, perhaps dozens of children were born on it!"

Leaving behind damasks, dark wood and Baroque paintings—except for a couple of still lifes in the sitting room—Nino has cast a spell of comfort and cosiness. It echoes his maternal family's modern sensibility, which now forms a shared lexicon with Paola. "I was taught to be open and curious rather than cling to ancient privileges." In his studio, the desk was commissioned by his grandfather, who had a knack for design (and aviation). The sunken blue chair was where his grandmother—a feminist *avant la lettre* who fled to Naples in the 1920s to study philosophy—used to sit.

On the other side of the house is Paola's studio. When not on the road reporting, she works in this snug room, surrounded by the tools of her trade and personal belongings, all within reach. Countless books—ranging from antique poetry volumes to entire anthologies of American literature—are piled up everywhere. Then Nino designed a library, and now, she muses, the shelves map the chronicles of her life and her family's story.

Clearly, this is home to two intellectuals, though their approaches may differ—his more aesthetic; hers more sentimental. Still, their collected possessions are like a Proustian madeleine to them both, infused with memories. "I get mad when something gets lost," Paola says. "Objects came before us and will outlive us."

By the late 19th-century safe cabinet in the entrance hall, a print of a Piranesi engraving of Rome is placed above the mirror, which reflects a screen print by Bruno Munari (*opposite*). On another wall hangs a décollage print by Mimmo Rotella depicting Marilyn Monroe (*left*). In the vaulted sitting room, the Eames rocking chair was a wedding gift (*above*). A view of the enfilade ends with a photograph of the Royal Palace of Caserta, north of Naples (*page 104*). Nino's grandmother's Poltrona Frau armchair dates from 1938 (*page 105*).

THE NEW YORKER

art of the sixties
from the ludwig museum the tel aviv museum may-july 1979

A reading corner in the dining room, featuring a lacquered credenza/sideboard and a Giorgio de Chirico drawing (*this page*). At the back is a white metal étagère designed by Nino (*opposite*). "There's real magic in dining in a space made for it, not in a hybrid setup with a sofa on one side," he says. Above the doorway to the sitting room is a rooster drawing by Salvatore Fiume that once belonged to his grandmother.

Etchings by Carlo Carrà in the dining room (*opposite*). The 20th-century kitchen, surmounted by a large hood, has been kept intact (*this page*). Nino's study is furnished with a 1930s chair and desk commissioned by his grandfather—his is also the historic issue of *Domus* magazine (*pages 110 and 111*). On the walls, a series of memorabilia: Nino's grandfather in aviator's uniform; his uncle, a fallen officer in World War II; his grandmother receiving a medal from Italy's postwar president Luigi Einaudi; vintage car catalogs and pictures featuring a model still in the family's possession.

JAGUAR
Cars
SERVICE
REPUBBLICA ITALIANA
MINISTERO DELLA DIFESA

UNDER SOUTHERN SKIES

It was the second day of the year, and Elena and Giulio were ready to start a new life. Leaving behind the city of Noto, the couple drove through a landscape rich with olive trees, citrus groves and vineyards. By the end of the day, they had stumbled upon a dilapidated farmhouse just sturdy enough to allow them to move in immediately.

Originally from Northern Italy, the two have known each other since childhood, but only fell in love a few years ago. Because they were living in different cities, they decided to escape to a third place—Sicily. "We both have roots in the island, so we knew it well," says Elena. "It just made sense with the kind of lifestyle that we wanted to have."

But the lifestyle they dreamed of proved to be hard work. The property was a remote one with no electricity, no water and not a soul in sight. "Just us and the sheep," Elena remembers. The couple began work on the land, planting trees and aromatic plants. Today, what was once a barren wasteland is a bucolic 30-acre/12-hectare dream, though not quite as they had visualized. "We did a business plan and realized that we would not be able to make a living from agriculture, so we veered to hospitality to sustain the farm," says Elena. Iuta Farm, as they named it, is now an eco-rural retreat with five safari-style tented lodges, four suites and a swimming pool surrounded by exotic vegetation.

Over the years, bit by bit, Elena and Giulio restored the unassuming-looking compound, including the former stable, where they eventually settled. And as their project grew, so did their family, with the arrival of baby son Marcello. The sustainable ethos with which they practice agrarian life and run their hospitality business is combined with an effortless elegance that's evident in every detail. "We didn't want to disturb," Elena explains. "We slowly tiptoed into this environment."

Upon entering the farm gate, the mood of this sunbaked oasis reveals itself. The soothing palette embraces earthy neutrals, echoing the tones of the coastal sandstone that was traditionally used to

DOROTHEA LANGE

Among the olive trees, a glimpse of the sandstone building housing the fireplace room (*page 112*). The outdoor kitchen, beneath a pergola made of bamboo canes, features a large convivial table crafted by Elena and Giulio from Etna chestnut wood planks on a metal base (*page 113*). On the table sits a bouquet of dried cardoons. This corner of the fireplace room features a low built-in sofa, a 1960s table lamp and a terracotta vase by Sternbach Interior Stories (*opposite*). A relaxed seating area shelters beneath a centuries-old olive tree, just one of many that cover the landscape of the hilly Val di Noto region (*right*). Almonds, citrus and various other fruits are also grown on the farm.

build the local *tonnare* (tuna fisheries). Concrete in matching shades covers the massive, almost brutalist walls of the old farmhouse. Inside, all is simple and warm. Light pours from the large windows into spartan yet chic bedrooms. The same minimal mood continues in the lofty, tranquil salon, which features a built-in sofa, a piano and a floating fireplace.

Scattered throughout are decorative pieces—from chairs to blankets—crafted in Morocco. "During a trip to Marrakech, we discovered multiple similarities between here and there, especially in terms of craftsmanship," says Elena. "The difference is that here, artisans are disappearing." The couple have surrounded themselves with items that exude softness and tactility. "You feel that North Africa is not far away, especially in the hot season when you have bare soil and everything turns golden."

The kitchen was designed by Elena with practicality in mind, although she admits that she was something of a novice when it came to cooking: "I had to throw away dozens of cakes to start, but now it's my forte." Meals are prepared using food grown on the farm or simple ingredients sourced from fellow locals: tomatoes, zucchini/courgettes, onions, figs and homemade ricotta.

Life here has reached a good balance. For half the year the family is surrounded by visitors, while the rest of the time it's just the three of them plus their animal family (two dogs and four cats). "There is work to do in every season, but you follow the rhythm of nature." Elena reflects that this lifestyle has made her reconsider her priorities; the things that once seemed important are no longer so. Nor does she need to consult her phone for the weather forecast. "You just look at the sky." The star-studded southern sky.

The sitting area on the veranda is often used for breakfast (*right*). Simple and cosy, it features a wicker sofa and iron coffee table adorned with majolica tiles from a second-hand dealer in Palermo. The staircase leads to the terrace, where sunset *aperitivi* can be enjoyed overlooking the citrus grove.

A sitting area framed by bougainvillea overlooks a small, private heated pool (*opposite*). The window surround was salvaged from an ancient manor. Scandi simplicity and artisanal touches come together in this outdoor space, featuring a coffee table by Danish brand Madam Stoltz and handcrafted wood and rope chairs from Morocco (*above*).

The fireplace, made by Elena and Giulio, has a suspended hood and recessed hearth in the concrete floor (*this page*). A corner of one of the suites, featuring an armchair from Morocco and a painting by Júlia Martins Miranda, a Brazilian artist based in Noto (*opposite*).

One of the armchairs commissioned in Morocco, upholstered in Akhnif fabric (*above*). In the kitchen, the custom-built pantry cabinet is fitted with reclaimed doors sourced from a carpenter on Mount Etna (*above right*). The iron knobs were salvaged from a flea market in Palermo. A detail of the kitchen's majolica tiles (*right*). A view of the dining room showcases a solid chestnut wood table from Etna paired with director's chairs by Telami and a cabinet found at a second-hand dealer in Avola (*opposite*).

DOROTHEA LANGE
SERGIO FIORENTINO

The bedrooms are monastic in design but feature a wealth of textural details; here an old Persian rug, an heirloom from Giulio's family, and a kalanchoe plant in a terracotta jar (*opposite*). A custom-designed sofa is upholstered in sage green linen, while the bench is by Madam Stoltz. Another terracotta jar, this one found at the market in Modica, holds dried giant fennel heads (*this page*). A rattan headboard, rustic rug and raffia bench complete the scene.

The staircase leading to the terrace (*this page*). At the heart of the sanctuary is the saltwater pool, one of the first elements completed upon Elena and Giulio's arrival (*opposite*). It is surrounded with sun loungers, tables and parasols by Atmosphera. The planting includes Mediterranean aromatics, such as rosemary, and other exotic plants thriving under the dazzling Sicilian sun.

The main building melds seamlessly with the landscape,its walls painted in earthy plaster (*this page*). It is surrounded by lush vegetation, including agaves, palms and clusters of giant birds of paradise (*Strelitzia reginae*). The lounge chairs are by Lafuma.

A LONG STORY

Naples, according to the Italian writer Curzio Malaparte, is the only city of the ancient world that "did not perish like Ilium, like Nineveh, like Babylon." It stands on pre-Christian foundations and many eras are layered in its modern image. Palazzo Spinelli di Laurino is no exception.

With its unique oval-shaped courtyard adorned with stucco bas-reliefs and statues perched above a Baroque staircase dating to the 18th century and another 15th-century staircase, once walked by horses, the palazzo stands as one of the most magnificent—yet decaying—examples of architecture in Naples. Here lives the writer and publisher Nathalie Heidsieck de Saint Phalle.

The daughter of two Parisian avant-garde artists linked to the Beat Generation, Nathalie grew up on Île Saint-Louis—"neither *rive gauche*, nor *rive droite*"—before heading to the Middle East as a reporter. She landed in Naples in the early 1990s to print a book in support of Balkan populations during the Yugoslav Wars. But while she awaited the copies, the press was sold, and retrieving them turned into a quest that spanned years. She found herself trapped in Naples, and with very little money but the help of friends, she moved into an apartment at Palazzo Spinelli: "It was a seedy, desolate space previously inhabited by a young couple," she says. "Both men died from AIDS—such was that era."

Painting the walls white—a little each day—became a sort of ritual to get through a gloomy time. "There was nothing in the house, so I photocopied the covers of my books and pinned them on the walls." After a while, the place came

THE GODS
THE GODS
AND THE GODS
ALL CAME
COURAGE,
APRÈS C'EST FINI !*

The living room is filled with artworks by the creatives who took part in Nathalie's Albergo del Purgatorio project (*pages 130–131*). From left to right, and top to bottom, this gallery wall features works by NHPSP, John Giorno, Paolo Berardinelli, Paolo Stampa, John Giorno, Christophe Tarkos, Joël Ducorroy, Paul-Armand Gette, Jean Degottex, Françoise Janicot, Jean Degottex, Salvatore Puglia, Françoise Janicot, Beatrice Caracciolo, patrickandrédepuis1966, Sébastien de Ganay, Alain Snyers and Jean Dupuy. A view from above of the palazzo's courtyard with 18th-century sculptures by Jacopo Cestaro (*opposite*). A bust of Graziella (a character from an 1852 novel by Alphonse de Lamartine) alongside works by Eric Morin and Salvatore Puglia (*below*).

together through gifts from friends, furniture left on the street and things found on her travels. "I'd buy a single pillow, a cap, whatever I liked. Nothing matched," she says. Often visiting Iran, she started trading in ancient rugs. "I developed an eye and ended up a collector. I used rugs to cover every inch of the floor (which had been redone in the 80s with dreadful cheap tiles)—like in a mosque."

Through word of mouth, colleagues and artist friends began visiting and praising the attractions of Naples, of which Nathalie had become an advocate. At one point, her phone number even appeared in *The New York Times*—"I'd find messages in my voicemail from people in Tokyo asking if they could book a room. A room? I barely had a mattress!"

An architect friend suggested renovating a space in another grand building, Palazzo Marigliano, creating three guest rooms: one opulent, one eccentric and one for those of lesser means, plus a student dormitory. Named Albergo del Purgatorio, it was the invented home of an imaginary traveler and collector, Robert Kaplan. The project expanded to include a gallery and club beneath Nathalie's Palazzo Spinelli apartment, where artists' works were presented as part of Kaplan's collection. Every day an *aperitivo* brought together people from radically different social classes and viewpoints.

Not long ago, all this came to an end, but Nathalie, who has split her life between Paris and Naples, continues to host visitors in her apartment: "When I was little, my sister often slept in my bed because someone else was using hers. Probably, someone is sleeping in my bed now."

After renovating a few spaces in this city—each time confronting the wear of time and bureaucracy—she is not sure this can go on. "Having studied Egyptology, I understand and love ruins. But at some point, things may fall down—and it could be just time to invent something else."

A work by French artist Françoise Janicot, Nathalie's mother, hangs on the wall in the living room above a white and green chair by Pierre Sala and Kurdish rugs (*above*). For a period, Nathalie traded in carpets, and now most of the floors are fully covered, as in a mosque—seen here are kilims from Anatolia and Iran and a Kurdish carpet (*right*). A corner of the salon features a work by Charlotte Moorman and voile curtains imported from India and dyed in Lyon, which Nathalie added soon after she arrived here (*opposite*).

CABLES
Y GARANTIES

WORK
OF
THE MOST
DISHONEST
ARTIST
EVER MET

comment ça va ?
MAIS ENCORE ?
SOYONS PRÉCIS
j'aime mieux !
comme vous y allez !
n'exagérons rien
mais encore
vous n'êtes pas graphiste que je sache !!!
Prétentieux de surcroît..
C'EST SI DIFFICILE !
et elle s'affiche
arrêtez votre Disque

A Piranha chair by Pierre Sala and works by Robert Kaplan, TLuise and Giuseppe Zevola in the hallway (*opposite above left and right*). The table in the guest bedroom was made by Claudio Catanese using glass salvaged from the wreckage of a jewelry-store window (*opposite below left*). Hanging on the wall here and above the bed are works by Françoise Janicot, Christophe Berhault, Nathalie's father Bernard Heidsieck and Brigitte Laffaille (*opposite below right*). Back in the hallway, a work by Philip Heying, Iranian kilims and a Kurdish carpet (*this page*).

Another Iranian kilim in the main bedroom with some of the many books found throughout the house, including those left behind by guests (*above*). Next to the bed, a work by Anette Lenz and a ceramic tile bearing the number 23—a memento of the time when the gallery below Nathalie's home opened a new exhibition on the 23rd of each month (*opposite*). On the wall hangs a silk rug from La Belle du Seigneur, produced in the mountains of Kashmir.

(IT'S) THE
MOMENT
COURAGE
COURAGE
COURAGE
23.

In the only room where the cement floor tiles remain, the walls still bear the imprint of the wallpaper that was removed, leaving behind an almost painterly effect (*pages 140 and 141*). Decorating the space are works by Françoise Janicot, Brigitte Laffaille, Maria de Morais, Raffaella Nappi, Paolo Stampa and Beatrice Caracciolo. The desk was made by Nathalie herself and the wooden chair behind it is from Africa. An Uzbek suzani covers the bed and a Kurdish carpet serves as a bedside rug. The work on the nightstand/bedside table is by Nathalie's father. Nathalie spends much of her time on the terrace during summer, especially reading (*above and opposite*). Occasionally, she has even slept there beneath the open sky.

FREE REIN

With its fortress-like features and faded palette, this former hunting lodge exudes a quiet theatricality reminiscent of a Wes Anderson film. Tucked away in the Sicilian countryside near Ragusa, on the edge of a protected nature reserve, it stands as the focal point at the end of a long driveway, among the blossoming almond groves and majestic carob trees.

The lodge is flanked by two outbuildings: a *palmento* (a structure once used for crushing grapes) and a guardian's house, both rebuilt from ruins. When the owners—a couple of Milan-based managers, with Sicilian roots on her side—came across the place, it was, in fact, a dismal scene. They immediately called on their friend the architect Roberto Gerosa, who faithfully restored the main house, had the *palmento* dismantled and reassembled stone by stone, and reimagined the interiors to be sympathetic to modern needs.

By any measure, conjuring a place to live is never straightforward. "Make things that are functional but at the same time have memory," says Roberto. "That, I believe, is the essence of a residential project." Still, starting from scratch can become an opportunity—a blank canvas on which the past can be reinvented. In search of a leitmotif to bring the interiors to life, he turned to local heritage. Known in Italy as *stile Liberty*, after the London department store, Art Nouveau was one of the most influential artistic movements in Sicily in the early 20th century, leaving a lasting imprint on the island's architecture and decorative arts. Drawing on these historic threads, Roberto wove them into the very fabric of the house.

A sculptural staircase anchors the layout, connecting the main level with a mezzanine above. Its iron and glass handrail reinterprets Liberty-era motifs and is painted in a muted shade inspired by the oxidized copper of Hector Guimard's entrances to the Paris Métro. The lightbulb moment came while Roberto was working with a Sicilian blacksmith. "You

The hallway, which also serves as a dining room, features a custom-made oval table with an opaline top and Liberty-style armchairs — a nod to the region's predominant architectural style (*page 144 left*). A 1970s French wall lamp in gilded and painted metal (*page 144 right*). The Liberty-inspired staircase, painted in an oxidized copper shade like the Paris Métro, was designed by Roberto Gerosa (*page 145*). The gymnastics horse was a gift from him to the homeowners. He also designed the terrazzo-topped kitchen table, which was made by Pavimenti Sansone in Comiso (*above and opposite*). A set of 1970s Swedish teak chairs is teamed with linen seat pads by Italtessil. The drawer fronts are made of crumpled brass; overhead is a brass and opaline lamp by Roberto.

know what I mean—you've been to Paris, right?" he asked, caught up in the fervor of creation. The man looked puzzled, but matched the colour with uncanny precision. Etched doors with frosted glass were salvaged from elsewhere, though they date back to the same period, as do the mahogany chairs.

An architect who also sees himself as an artisan, and with a background in creative direction, Roberto focuses on the expressive touches that shape a space's mood. With an aesthetic sensibility attuned to the whimsical, he brought something unexpected to the foyer: two diminutive donkeys crafted from jute. Throughout the house, he softens thresholds and canopy beds with flowing fabrics. But his true signature lies in the lamps he fabricates in his Milanese atelier, fashioning them from copper wire, brass, opaline, silk and even parchment. He has been making them since the 1980s, when Diane von Fürstenberg walked into a gallery in New York and said: "I want that moon!"—referring to one of his moon-shaped designs. Slightly oversized, they hang from the ceiling or settle into corners, adding a storybook charm.

Underfoot, powdery-toned stone from nearby Comiso is paired with pitch-black *pietra pece*, both chiseled by hand. Craftsmanship was key to achieving the level of material detail Roberto envisioned—seen, for instance, in the kitchen: in the terrazzo tabletop made with chips of both types of stone and green glass; in the crumpled brass sheet metal used for the drawer fronts; and in the cast Baroque-style pantry door handles. The room radiates a twisted, old-school Southern allure, blending utilitarian and more opulent objects—a vintage red kettle, wicker baskets, Sicilian ceramic jars, silver trays, a slate board—all arranged with effortless style.

On the day of our visit, Roberto is in the kitchen surrounded by the saturated hues of early spring vegetables from the countryside, cooking and serving a salad the Sicilian way—with ripened tomatoes and pungent onions. More often than not, he ends up becoming a friend to his clients. "Helping them understand what they really need leads me to develop a very close relationship with them," he explains. "In truth, it often happens that some of my clients even end up becoming interior decorators themselves."

Here, he says, his job isn't finished yet. He keeps returning, adding things, shifting others—and maintaining that delicate balance between refinement and domesticity.

-SIDA
H^2O

In the library, the sofa is covered in Balinese ikat fabric that echoes the tones of the Indian kilim rug (*opposite*). Hanging above is a silk lamp by Roberto. In the corner is a Franklin stove in coral finish. The series of prints on the wall is by Giuseppe Colombo. A plaster sculpture of *Giuditta* by Dino Cunsolo is displayed alongside a series of vintage silver bromide photographs reproducing Antonio Canova's marbles (*above*).

In a cozy corner of the sitting room, a custom-designed sofa upholstered in heavy gold linen with contrasting borders by Italtessil stands next to a Rococo-style display cabinet in green and gold wood (*above left*). Davide Groppi's Calvino table lamp in steel and brass (*above right*). A sweeping view of the sitting room, framed by a ceiling with Catalan vaults and softened by a Moroccan wool rug on the floor, with Napoleon III-style chairs (*opposite*). Paintings by Giovanni La Cognata depict local architecture, including the nearby city of Comiso. The wooden sculpture on the coffee table is by Sebastiano Messina. The ceiling fan was made by Faro Barcelona.

the world
the world

The twin bedroom, which overlooks the serene countryside through a small window, perfectly exemplifies Roberto's talent for designing theatrical spaces with the charm of dollhouse rooms (*right*). The floral fantasy of the pouf contrasts with the striped vintage Italian iron four-poster beds, draped in period fabrics sourced from an antiques market. A salmon-pink silk pendant lamp with a copper structure, crafted by Roberto, gently illuminates the space, enhancing the room's nostalgic atmosphere.

A view of the architecture with a Wes Anderson-like feel, featuring shutters in an oxidized copper tone and graced by the presence of a lemon tree heavy with fruit (*opposite*). On the roof terrace, a collection of vintage glazed terracotta vases from Santo Stefano di Camastra, near Messina, sits at each corner. A detail of the indoor fireplace in the sitting room captures the light at day's end (*right*). Looking from the roof toward the back of the house, an expansive view opens onto the agricultural estate planted with olive, carob, and almond trees. A pool, inspired by traditional animal troughs, lies on the opposite side of the property, discreetly hidden from the driveway.

VAULTING AMBITION

It was entirely by chance rather than design that architect and collector Luca Bombassei landed in Puglia. He was invited to attend the opening of a whimsical *trullo* owned by a couple of friends and soon realized he was hooked. To his surprise, Luca was captivated by "the energy of the region, with that incredibly charming red soil and the most intriguing Baroque architecture."

Another *trullo* was available right next to his friend's house, and he immediately closed the deal. But a few years later, Luca began considering a move to a larger home. "I wanted," he says, "a space big enough to welcome friends and to showcase the works of artists I've collected."

In the town of Nardò, close to the coast, Luca stumbled upon a relic of rural life—a ruined *masseria*. These traditional fortified farmhouses, typical of the region, were owned by local landowners and occupied year-round by farmers who lived downstairs, next to the animals. The upper floors were opened only when the owners retreated to their country estates for the summer. Above the main entrance, the faded coat of arms of the original owners still remains.

Crossing the threshold, you catch a glimpse of the space enclosed within the walls—a wide courtyard known as the *tumara*, or place where livestock grazes. Two majestic carob trees stand at its center, surrounded by a fragrant carpet of rosemary, thyme, oregano and myrtle.

Although the property is listed, with some parts dating back to the 16th century, it had been left to fall into disrepair; vandalized and covered with graffiti. "Somehow, that was the ideal starting point, as it allowed me to restore everything to its original condition," Luca explains. "I wanted to preserve as much as possible and leave the patina untouched."

Works were carried out according to local tradition: the corners of the house are constructed from large tuff stones, while the floor is finished in smooth *cocciopesto*, made from

The main entrance is at the front of the house (*page 156 above right*). The porch is furnished with a rare Carlo Scarpa table for Simon and chairs by Afra and Tobia Scarpa for Molteni, all dating from the 1970s (*page 156 below left*). Once a shelter for livestock, the deep portico is now a winter garden and home to Rodolfo Dordoni's Eden modular sofa for RODA and an antique wicker chaise longue (*page 157*). A glimpse into the kitchen (*left*). In the foreground, a self-portrait by Keith Haring, dated 1980 and executed in marker pen on a notepad, hangs on the wall—one of the many artworks collected by the homeowner. The custom-designed cabinetry is by Luca Bombassei Studio and includes a convivial counter paired with Zara Home stools. Another view of the kitchen, showcasing a combination of brass and oak wood with a carbon-stained finish (*opposite*). The Niceta pendant light suspended above the sink is by Afra and Tobia Scarpa for Flos. A carefully curated selection of vases is displayed on the counter, including antique local pottery and minimalist white ceramic pieces by Bruno Gambone from the 1970s.

lime and crushed terracotta. It's a construction material that dates back to the Romans, yet the furnishings are decidedly 20th century. "I wanted to avoid the cliché of a rustic holiday *masseria*," Luca muses. "So I filled the space with design pieces by masters like Ettore Sottsass, Carlo Scarpa and Alessandro Mendini. It was considered unconventional here at the time, but it felt true to me."

Raised between Milan and Venice in a family of entrepreneurs, Luca was expected to follow the same path. Studying architecture was his way of breaking away. Today, he heads a Milan-based practice specializing in the restoration of historic houses. Luca has been an avid collector since his twenties, and many of his clients rely on his expertise in designing homes around art.

Contemporary artworks are scattered throughout, including large-scale pieces such as the site-specific blue and yellow work by Swiss artist Olivier Mosset painted on the roof. "I wanted this place to fit the context and feel suspended in time, so I hid all the elements that seemed out of place." However, it's possible to walk on the roof—inside the artwork—while gazing at the ancient pigeon tower in the distance. All these diverse elements come together organically.

On the long terrace once used to collect rainwater for the cistern, the original well provides an architectural centerpiece. How such a piece—a slice of neoclassical colonnade—found itself in this rural landscape is perhaps best explained by the story Luca imagines: "I pictured a lord traveling to Rome and bringing back a piece from his Grand Tour, like a souvenir, for his town."

The property overlooks a grove of olives, their silvery leaves gleaming in the sunlight. When Luca started the renovation, a disease began ravaging the trees around the house, leaving a desolate landscape. Determined to restore what was lost, he has since planted 6,000 young trees—not bad for a city dweller!

DELLA SERA

The south-facing den is part of an enfilade of rooms with cross- and star-vaulted ceilings (*opposite*). The artwork on the wall is *Pip* by Adelaide Cioni, while the wicker magazine rack is by Franco Campo and Carlo Graffi. This room also features a 17th-century fireplace with its original patina (*this page*). The mantel is home to a collection of vintage mirrors, glass vases by Jochen Holz and Murano glass candleholders in the form of fishes by Alessandro Palver. The Milord armchairs are by Marco Zanuso.

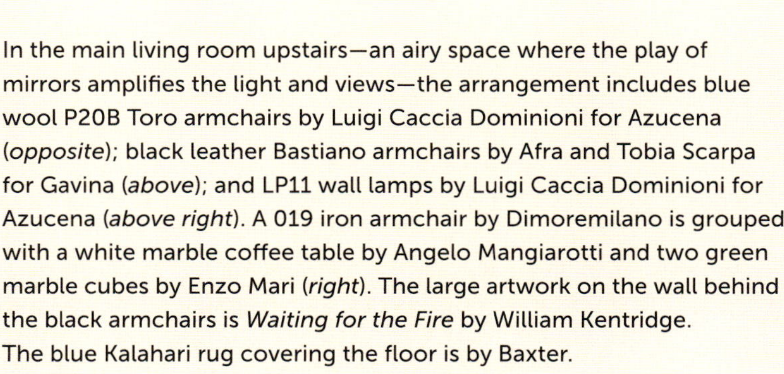

In the main living room upstairs—an airy space where the play of mirrors amplifies the light and views—the arrangement includes blue wool P20B Toro armchairs by Luigi Caccia Dominioni for Azucena (*opposite*); black leather Bastiano armchairs by Afra and Tobia Scarpa for Gavina (*above*); and LP11 wall lamps by Luigi Caccia Dominioni for Azucena (*above right*). A 019 iron armchair by Dimoremilano is grouped with a white marble coffee table by Angelo Mangiarotti and two green marble cubes by Enzo Mari (*right*). The large artwork on the wall behind the black armchairs is *Waiting for the Fire* by William Kentridge. The blue Kalahari rug covering the floor is by Baxter.

One of the bedrooms is partly painted with a burgundy lacquer accent to enhance the contrast with the patina of the original plaster (*opposite*). On the wall is *Mirror* by Maurizio Donzelli; the rosewood credenza/sideboard is Danish and the white armchair is by Gio Ponti. Beneath the 18th-century star-vaulted ceilings of the dining room stands a 1970s Samo marble table by Carlo Scarpa, Catilina chairs by Luigi Caccia Dominioni for Azucena and a Plexi 1 pendant light by Angelo Mangiarotti (*this page*).

In the sitting room, the original *cocciopesto* floor has been preserved (*above left and right*). A Mario Schifano artwork, *Untitled*, hangs above the Baxter Leon sofa, complemented by a gilded metal coffee table and a couple of Gio Ponti armchairs upholstered in petrol blue satin. A watercolor by Lucia Veronesi hangs near the window. Other artworks include *Vaso Natura* by Lucia Pescador in the foreground, while *Chaos* by Sun Xue hangs on the back wall (*opposite*).

The downstairs master bedroom features locally produced *cocciopesto* flooring and a reclaimed 19th-century door (*right*). The bed is by Luca Bombassei Studio, behind which is a 1980s screen from Alessandro Mendini's Ollo series. Hanging above the bed is a TRN Light D20 ceramic pendant by Pani Jurek. The black lacquered nightstand by Willy Rizzo is home to a table lamp by Marion Duclos Mailaender, while the wicker easy chair is by Franco Albini and dates from 1964.

The *tumara*, or courtyard, is planted with carob trees and aromatic plants (*this page*). On the terrace, the architect installed a table made of reclaimed tuff stone and wrought-iron chairs, all designed by Luca Bombassei Studio (*page 172*). The neoclassical-style structure is a well for collecting rainwater. Beyond, an olive grove stretches into the landscape. A group of Tripolina chairs surrounds a table repurposed from a circular mirror, in front of *Ayia Rakaya*, a textile work by artist Ibrahim Mahama (*page 173 above left*). Other images showcase locally crafted ceramics, a riad-inspired corner with tiles designed by the owner and a secluded pool (*above right and below*).

A NEW CHAPTER

Giuseppe Amato had always wanted to be an artist. But when the time came to choose a university, his mother—an artist herself—warned him about the precarious nature of an artistic life. So, Giuseppe went on to study biology instead.

However, during a marine research expedition, he found himself far more intrigued by the boat's features than by the ocean life deep beneath it. He began fantasizing about boat-like houses, and his daydreams didn't go unnoticed by his fellow students. "Are you sure," they asked, "that you want to be a marine biologist?"

It turned out that Giuseppe didn't, and what followed was his transformation into a self-taught cabinetmaker. One day, he discovered that the master at the local workshop was leaving. Determined to replace him, Giuseppe claimed to have experience in woodwork, while in fact he would study each night, then on the following day teach others what he had just learned. Today an artist and designer, he's certainly something of a modern Renaissance man.

Giuseppe first moved to this apartment in Palermo's Art Nouveau quarter during childhood, when his father—a lawyer—converted part of it into an office by dividing the space with a 1960s bookcase. "Through it, I could hear the clients arguing in Sicilian dialect," he recalls, amused. At that time, the place didn't feel like home to him. His mother had moved to Rome, to begin a new life with the writer and philosopher Ruggero Guarini, and Giuseppe often traveled to the capital to visit her and her new partner, who was to become something of a mentor to him. Then a piano was delivered to the Palermo apartment, his fiancée began to visit him there and he finally made peace with his surroundings.

Recently, Giuseppe, who is now based in Milan but frequently returns to Sicily, decided to renovate the apartment. To begin with, he removed the mid-century bookcase. This immediately opened up the space, allowing the eye to

007
173
050
018
025
033
032

The plaster moldings/cornices on the walls are original to the apartment, as are the floor tiles, which date back to the Art Nouveau era and feature a different design in each room, including the dining area (*pages 174 and 175*). A 1960s Arco lamp by Achille and Pier Giacomo Castiglioni for Flos curves over a smoked glass André table by Tobia and Afra Scarpa for Gavina. The domed shade tones with steel-framed Cesca chairs by Marcel Breuer. By the entrance hangs a slate blackboard that Giuseppe carries with him to every house he completes (*opposite*). A vintage opaline glass lamp sits beneath a tempera-on-panel painting by Rodolfo Loffredo, Giuseppe's uncle (*below right*).

wander through the enfilade of rooms. At the center is the living room/library, flanked by two bedrooms. The rest of the apartment is laid out along a second axis, with another bedroom, two bathrooms and a fully renovated kitchen, designed to feel like it has always been there.

The apartment is a calm, cosy space, with walls painted in shades of gray reminiscent of a Vermeer and spruced up with a coat of lime putty. "I have faith in lime putty," says Giuseppe. "It's what keeps up structures like the Pantheon in Rome. It ages beautifully." The rooms are furnished with a mosaic of inherited pieces: a dresser/chest of drawers from Giuseppe's mother's family stands alongside furniture that his father acquired, such as a carved oak bed by Ernesto Basile, "the architect who made Palermo." They sit in harmony beside the Rationalist pieces selected by Heidi, his father's Swiss partner, whom he met after divorcing Giuseppe's mother.

But the true soul of the home is without a doubt the library, which lines the walls of the living space. "When I was just beginning as a cabinetmaker—crafting a mahogany canoe, of which I was immensely proud—clients would step into my workshop and exclaim, 'Ah, Mr. Amato, what a beautiful canoe you've made! Could you make me a library?'" Giuseppe has created all kinds of libraries for passionate bibliophiles, but this is the first one he's made for himself, and it's also the simplest, consisting of minimalist metal shelves covering the walls. "When empty, it might look a bit odd, but filled with books, it comes alive," he enthuses.

Both his father's and his mentor's books have found a home here, and it is evident that Giuseppe treasures the memories of these charismatic figures. "You know, they were polar opposites," he recalls with a smile, "with incompatible tastes and interests—oh, what spirited debates they had!"

The stainless-steel kitchen, handcrafted for Giuseppe by LG Tech, is complemented by Scintilla wall lights by Piero and Livio Castiglioni (*this page*). The space is defined by the contrast between black and white: a Carrara marble-topped table is paired with satin-finish metal chairs by Harry Bertoia for Knoll. An artisanal prototype of a pendant light completes the setting (*opposite*).

In the living room, the long wooden table was created by Giuseppe for reading and working, while the Parentesi lamps are by Achille Castiglioni and Pio Manzù for Flos (*opposite*). This space is home to a floor-to-ceiling library, its metal shelving designed and made by Giuseppe with a focus on simplicity and economy. The numbers burned into wooden plaques indicate the organization of the books. With its collection of 10,000 volumes, the library stretches across the walls of adjoining rooms, becoming a defining motif—the residence even takes its name from it, Liberty Library. A terracotta sculpture, created by Giuseppe when he was a boy, and other collected items (*above left and right*).

The living-room window offers a glimpse of Palermo's Politeama-Libertà district, a charming pocket of the city where Art Nouveau architecture stands in well-preserved splendor (*this page*). The apartment is just a short walk from the city's main theaters. One end of the living area features a 1960s leather sofa, Marcel Breuer's iconic Wassily chairs and an Eero Saarinen Tulip table for Knoll (*opposite*).

142
141
DUMAS
STALIN
168
089
062
124
085
083
LA SECONDA GUERRA MONDIALE
076

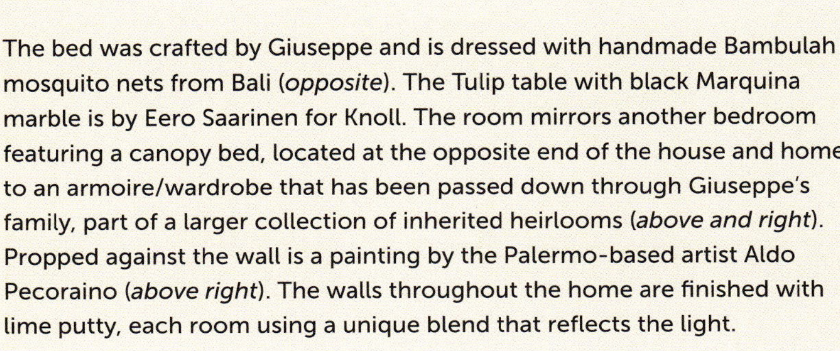

The bed was crafted by Giuseppe and is dressed with handmade Bambulah mosquito nets from Bali (*opposite*). The Tulip table with black Marquina marble is by Eero Saarinen for Knoll. The room mirrors another bedroom featuring a canopy bed, located at the opposite end of the house and home to an armoire/wardrobe that has been passed down through Giuseppe's family, part of a larger collection of inherited heirlooms (*above and right*). Propped against the wall is a painting by the Palermo-based artist Aldo Pecoraino (*above right*). The walls throughout the home are finished with lime putty, each room using a unique blend that reflects the light.

In one of the three bedrooms, a carved bed made of oak dates back to the early 1900s (*this page*). Discovered by Giuseppe, it is a piece by Ernesto Basile, the Sicilian architect and a leading figure of modernism and the Liberty style. The nightstands are by Rodolfo Loffredo, the owner's uncle. The 19th-century cane rocking chair is by Thonet (*opposite*).

JOURNEY'S END

Nini Bonavoglia's house in Valle d'Itria is a delightful blend of Mediterranean ease, International style and Berber flair—the product of his nomadic nature. He has returned to Puglia after many years spent living abroad and an intricate web of travels spanning from South America to North Africa. In truth, he says, he feels at home nowhere, yet he is content anywhere.

At eighteen, Nini fled his childhood home for Milan, where he discovered the pleasures of art, and then New York, where he went on to study the art market. What was meant to be a brief academic detour—ten months to write his thesis—effortlessly turned into ten years. This was followed by six years in London, where he founded his art consultancy firm Repertorio.

Nini was travelling across Patagonia in 2020 when the pandemic hit, and he decided it was time to return to Puglia; if not to settle down, at least to establish a house. He weighed up a series of *masserie* in the southern part of the region, each grander than the last, and in the end, he opted for a plot of land within easy reach of his hometown Bari, the region's capital. His grandson had just been born, and he wanted to spend more time with the family.

A location in the countryside, as isolated as possible, was his principal requirement. "After years in the city, I craved nature," Nini says. In this he has succeeded. To get to his new home, one has to leave Ostuni—the so-called White City, perched on a hill—and drive down a narrow track lined with dry-stone walls. "Here lie the remains of

In the main living room, a Belgian sofa anchors a mix of modern design and rustic elements (*pages 188–189*). Ceramic works by Nini Bonavoglia are scattered across surfaces, including *Overthinking*, a male head resting on a rough worktable. The photograph on the wall is by Alessio Boni. In the main bedroom, a 19th-century portrait hangs on a bespoke metal wall that screens the closet and bathroom (*below*). The Camaleonda modular seat at the foot of the bed is a 1970s design by Mario Bellini for B&B Italia (*opposite left*). In the second living room, an old Berber bowl rests on a stack of books (*opposite right*). This space is arranged around a cinnamon-toned Carrera sofa by De Pas, D'Urbino and Lomazzi for BBB Italia, with an artwork by Jakub Milčák on the wall (*pages 192 and 193*). The ceramic handles on the rustic built-in cabinet were made by Nini.

medieval *trulli Saraceni* and two structures that were probably used for agricultural storage," he explains.

Around the house, the olive-dotted Puglian landscape gives way to a planting of grasses and succulents—a wild tableau visible from indoors and framed by the large openings carved into the solid volumes of the two preserved and expanded buildings. "No tiny windows here," he says. The *trulli* have become part of the complex, their organic forms absorbed into the geometry. Their rough surfaces are thick with plaster, like cream cakes baking under the sun.

Nini worked on the project with his sister Francesca, an architect who also lives in the region. The warm, earthy interiors, which seem to gain depth through a sort of *chiaroscuro* effect, reflect his own sense of drama and intimacy. He explains how he played with contrasts: "The juxtaposition of sunlit surfaces and deep shadows adds a sculptural quality to the space and enhances texture."

Shiny velvet, aged wood and coarse raffia create a stark contrast with the raw metal accents, industrial in spirit, which he subtly introduced through window frames and furnishings, such as side-tables with tops clad in *maiolica* tiles. A metal grid covers an entire wall in his moody bedroom (it hides a closet and screens the access to a striped granite bathroom). "I wanted something intensely masculine to sharpen this rustic setting," he explains. The handles, by contrast, are delicate ceramic objects crafted by the owner himself. The grid is also "the perfect backdrop for hanging paintings"—on it hangs a 19th-century male torso, modest but charged with pathos, which he bought at auction.

Nini's involvement with ceramics is a recent but sweeping affair. He was in Paris when he first put his hands in clay, attending a workshop just around the corner from a friend's house. Two weeks were enough to get him

hooked and, by the time he returned to Italy, he had bought a kiln. He turned out to be a natural. "It's an incredibly slow and meditative activity," he says. "You learn by doing—by getting it wrong. And the progress that comes after a mistake can be truly surprising."

The timing was ideal—as the space was taking shape, he began to weave his own work into it: the lighting, the vases and the fireplace are all his. The birth of the house thus coincided with his initiation as an artist. Resting on a workbench in the living room is one of his favorite sculptures—a vigorous blue and earthy brown head, on the verge of explosion, which he named *Overthinking*: a piece that channels volatile masculinity. He blends these figures, which carry an almost archaic quality and timeless vitality, with the classic examples of Italian design that he collects (including works by Franco Albini, Ignazio Gardella and Angelo Mangiarotti) and the contemporary artworks he has commissioned.

Among his collections, Nini has amassed mats from across the Maghreb, a region of North Africa inhabited by Berbers since long before the arrival of the Arabs in the seventh century. These traditional artifacts, woven from plant fibers sourced around the desert, are now scattered throughout the house, indoors and out, laid over the quartz and concrete floor that connects the spaces.

On one of them, Nini discovered the Amazigh glyph: a symbol of the olive tree and, in Berber culture, of the "free man." While the term Berber may derive from *barbarus*, the Latin for "foreigner," Amazigh is the name these nomads have chosen for themselves. It's also the name Nini has chosen for his far-flung house in the country.

One of the three kitchens of the house painted in warm, earthy plaster tones, offset by metal mesh elements that lend an industrial, masculine edge (*pages 194 and 195*). Gentle touches soften the dramatic ensemble, like the 18th-century Andalusian *maiolica* plate on the wall. The guest bedrooms feature elegant Venini appliqués (*above*). A ceramic lamp made by Nini rests on a small cabinet next to a cozy alcove with a built-in sofa (*right*). His entire home is punctuated with Italian design classics—here a bamboo armchair by Franco Albini for Bonacina by the bed is visible through the iron-framed windows that connect the interiors to the surrounding landscape (*opposite*).

Passionate about cooking—especially outdoors—Nini had an *al fresco* kitchen purpose-built beside a dining area (*right*). The table is made from old wooden beams and concrete and surrounded by 1950s wicker chairs by Franco Campo and Carlo Graffi. Breezy Andalusian mats serve as makeshift curtains—an ensemble that reflects Nini's laid-back lifestyle and desire to stay close to nature. The house was built around a pre-existing olive tree, which can be seen in the background.

The patio was poured in concrete, leaving space for existing trees and newly planted species. Tripolina chairs sit beneath a pergola in the relaxation area by the pool (*above*). At the pool's edge, vintage bamboo daybeds face the house (*above right*). The remains of ancient Saracen *trulli* have been integrated into the main structure and now house the guest bedrooms (*right*). The staircase leads to the rooftop, a favorite spot for *aperitivi*. Nini loves rescuing abandoned plants and give them a second life in his garden—they include the agave pictured here alongside rosemary and other sun-loving species that thrive in this Mediterranean patchwork (*opposite*).

PICTURE CREDITS

1 Project by Ludovica Serafini + Roberto Palomba—Palomba Serafini Associati; **2** Luca Bombassei, architect and collector, owner of Masseria Morice Grande, www.lucabombassei.com; **3** la melagrana/FCN 2009, architect Maria Giuseppina Grasso Cannizzo, www.la-melagrana.it; **4** ANM 2018, the home of Antonino Nicastro and Angela Bucello, architectural project by Maria Giuseppina Grasso Cannizzo; **5** IUTA Farm, Elena Cicciù and Giulio Costa with architect Paolo Costa, @iutafarm; **6** Project by Ludovica Serafini + Roberto Palomba—Palomba Serafini Associati; **7** la melagrana/FCN 2009, architect Maria Giuseppina Grasso Cannizzo, www.la-melagrana.it; **8** Liberty Library, la casa dei libri, artist and designer Giuseppe Amato, www.giuseppeamato.com; **9 left** Kaplan's Project; **9 right** Luca Bombassei, architect and collector, owner of Masseria Morice Grande, www.lucabombassei.com; **10–31** Villa Ruiz, architect Corrado Papa, www.fondazionedelgrandtour.it; **32–47** la melagrana/FCN 2009, architect Maria Giuseppina Grasso Cannizzo, www.la-melagrana.it; **48–63** Beylik, the home of Peter Benson Miller and Giovanni Panebianco, @peterbensonmiller; **64–79** Project by Ludovica Serafini + Roberto Palomba—Palomba Serafini Associati; **80–97** ANM 2018, the home of Antonino Nicastro and Angela Bucello, architectural project by Maria Giuseppina Grasso Cannizzo; **98–111** Architect Nino Filotico and journalist Paola Mos cardino, www.filoticoandpartners.com; **112–129** IUTA Farm, Elena Cicciù and Giulio Costa with architect Paolo Costa, @iutafarm; **130–143** Kaplan's Project; **144–155** Tenuta Aleppo Ragusa, architecture by Roberto Gerosa; **156–173** Luca Bombassei, architect and collector, owner of Masseria Morice Grande, www.lucabombassei.com; **174–187** Liberty Library, la casa dei libri, artist and designer Giuseppe Amato, www.giuseppeamato.com; **188–201** The home of artist Nini Bonavoglia in Puglia; **203** Luca Bombassei, architect and collector, owner of Masseria Morice Grande, www.lucabombassei.com; **204** Villa Ruiz, architect Corrado Papa, www.fondazionedelgrandtour.it; **205** Liberty Library, la casa dei libri, artist and designer Giuseppe Amato, www.giuseppeamato.com; **208** The home of artist Nini Bonavoglia in Puglia.

BUSINESS CREDITS

VILLA RUIZ
Fondazione del Grand Tour
www.fondazionedelgrandtour.it

Corrado Papa
Architect
www.architettocorradopapa.it
Pages 10–31; 204

MARIA GIUSEPPINA GRASSO CANNIZZO
Architect
mg.grassocannizzo@gmail.com

la melagrana/FCN 2009
www.la-melagrana.it
Pages 3; 7; 32–47

ANM 2018
With landscape project by
Federica Raggio
Pages 4; 80–97

BEYLIK
Ketty Di Tardo
Architect

Studio Ma0
www.ma0.it
Pages 48–63

LUDOVICA SERAFINI + ROBERTO PALOMBA
Architects

Palomba Serafini Associati
www.palombaserafini.com
Pages 1; 6; 64–79

NINO FILOTICO
Architect

Filotico and Partners
www.filoticoandpartners.com
Pages 98–111

IUTA FARM
www.iuta.farm

Paolo Costa
Architect
+39 0444 325032
Pages 5; 112–129

TENUTA ALEPPO RAGUSA
Roberto Gerosa
Architect
www.robertogerosa.eu
Pages 144–155

MASSERIA MORICE GRANDE
Luca Bombassei
Architect and collector
www.lucabombassei.com

Fiore Spagnolo Architetti
Architects
www.fiorespagnolo architetti.com
Pages 2; 9 right; 156–173; 203

GIUSEPPE AMATO
Artist and designer

Giuseppe Amato Studio
Artworks and architecture
www.giuseppeamato.com
Pages 8; 174–187; 205

NINI BONAVOGLIA
Artist
@ninibonavoglia

Francesca Bonavoglia
Architect
francesca.bonavoglia @gmail.com
Pages 188–201; 208

075
052
Poesie d'amore

INDEX

Page numbers in *italic* refer to the illustrations

ACKNOWLEDGMENTS

The writer and the photographer would like to express their deepest gratitude to each and every one of the homeowners and architects featured in these stories. We feel privileged to have had the chance to get to know you, your vision, and your homes so closely. It was enthralling, fun, at times even moving—and always inspiring.

To those who supported us throughout the process by giving advice, fact-checking, re-reading, traveling, cooking and so much more: Niccolò Bocci, Maddalena Bonicelli, Francesca Buscemi, Stefano Celesti, Francesca Ciuffreda, Giovanni Gasparini, Barbara Meneghel, Fabrizio Meris, Paola Messina, Rosario Midolo, Beatrice Rizzardi and Olimpia Rossi Bonato.

To the incredibly professional and endlessly patient team at RPS: special thanks to editor Sophie Devlin, creative director Leslie Harrington, head of production Patricia Harrington, senior designer Megan Smith and senior commissioning editor Annabel Morgan.

The publishers would also like to extend their thanks to everyone who graciously opened their homes to us.